Pg. 97

Fact Finders®

The Story of
Sanitation

TOILETS
TANK!

THEIR INNER
WORKINGS

by Riley Flynn

CAPSTONE PRESS
a capstone imprint

Fact Finder Books are published by Capstone Press,
1710 Roe Crest Drive, North Mankato, Minnesota 56003
www.mycapstone.com

Library of Congress Cataloging-in-Publication Data
Library of Congress Cataloging-in-Publication data is available on the Library of Congress website.

ISBN 978-1-5435-3114-5 (hardback)
ISBN 978-1-5435-3118-3 (paperback)
ISBN 978-1-5435-3122-0 (eBook PDF)

Editorial Credits
Anna Butzer, editor; Bobbie Nuytten, designer;
Morgan Walters, media researcher; Kris Wilfahrt, production specialist

Photo Credits
Alamy: GL Archive, 11, top 29, Splash News, 27; Getty Images: Tommy Olofsson, 16; iStockphoto:
Aksenovko, 8, BMPix, 9, daverhead, 25, bottom right 28; Newscom: Christiane Oelrich/dpa/
picture-alliance, 26; Shutterstock: AF studio, design element throughout, Africa Studio, 21, left 29,
Alessandro DYD, 22, bumbumbo, bottom right 20, Damian Palus, (toilet) Cover, Designua, 13,
Destiny VisPro, 24, HomeArt, 1, top right 29, I WALL, design element throughout, John_Dakapu,
18, Lek Changply, 19, Madhourse, 23, Margoe Edwards, 6, Milkovasa, 5, Mindscape studio,
(bathroom) Cover, 4, Moozartae, 17, Motorama, (sewer) Cover, Nik Symkin, bottom middle 20,
Oleksandr Lytvynenko, bottom left 20, Patchra Suttivirat, 15, Roman Tiraspolsky, 7, Tribalium, 12,
Vertes Edmond Mihai, left 28

Printed and bound in the United States
PA021

TABLE OF CONTENTS

CHAPTER 1
YOUR OWN SUPERBOWL

Toilets. We use them every day—at home, school, restaurants, shopping malls—but we rarely talk about them. We might not realize it, but the toilet might be one of the most important inventions of all time. Yet many of us take this common household item for granted.

The toilet handle in a public restroom can have up to 40,000 germs per square inch.

The average person uses the toilet about seven times per day. That adds up to 2,555 bathroom visits each year. Most of us probably take these trips to the bathroom without thinking twice, but what would happen if we didn't have a place to relieve ourselves?

The average modern toilet uses 1.6 gallons (6.1 liters) of water in a single flush.

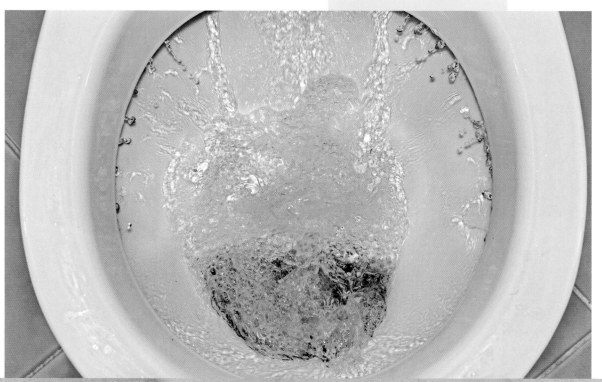

Life with Your Toilet

Think about your typical day. What is one of the first things you do in the morning after you wake up? What is one of the last things you do before you go to bed at night? Or maybe you drank too much lemonade before bed and wake up in the middle of the night? In each of these cases, you probably make your way down the hall to use the toilet. There is toilet paper, warm water to wash your hands, and maybe even be a soft rug on the floor.

Washing your hands prevents spreading illnesses to others.

Toilets are a luxury most of us have never had to live without. But imagine what your life would be like without the "porcelain throne." You might not have thought about it before, but admit it—life without your toilet would stink, to say the least!

CHAPTER 2

THE TOILET'S DIRTY HISTORY

Having a functional toilet in your home probably doesn't seem like a big deal. However, it wasn't always that way. The toilet as we know it hasn't been around very long. Just 150 years ago, people were living up close and personal with their poop.

These ancient public toilets are located in Rome.

The area where the waste traveled down was called the waste chute.

Thousands of years ago, a few civilizations had early versions of the toilet. In the 1900s BC, some Greeks had toilets in their homes. The Romans had public restrooms in the 100s In some of these restrooms, water ran through pipes to wash away waste. Some other restrooms had seats that were built over ditches filled with water.

These ancient toilets disappeared over time as the civilizations grew and changed. Before toilets were invented, people threw their waste into the streets or into nearby lakes and rivers. The germs in the waste created a lot of diseases, and many people became sick.

Royal Flush

In 1596 John Harrington came up with the idea of the flushing toilet. Harrington was a family friend of England's Queen Elizabeth I. Harrington designed the first toilet for the Queen. Harrington's plans were similar to the toilets we have today, but almost 300 years passed before the idea of the toilet really caught on.

FACT The first toilet was installed in the White House in 1825.

CLEAN COINCIDENCE

Between 1832 and 1849, a disease called cholera killed more than 150,000 Americans. Many scientists now believe that human waste in the food and water supplies caused the disease. This knowledge helped the toilet become even more popular.

In 1861 an English plumber named Thomas Crapper began trying to improve Harrington's designs. By the 1880s he was selling toilets to the public. Most of these toilets were simple bowls that whooshed away waste with a big flush of water. In most cities this waste flowed into large **cesspools**.

Only wealthy people could afford toilets in their homes at first. The most expensive part was piping wastewater away from homes. Eventually cities began building or improving their sewer systems. These systems of pipes carried waste away once a toilet was flushed. Public sewer systems also made toilets cheaper to install for everyone. It didn't take long for nearly every home in England and the United States to have a flushing toilet.

Thomas Crapper
(1836–1910)

cesspool—a pit in the ground that holds human waste and other garbage

CHAPTER 3

THE INS AND OUTS OF A TOILET

Waste seems to magically disappear when we flush the toilet. To find out how it works, we need to ask questions such as the following. Where does the water in the bowl come from? How does the flush handle work? Where does all the wastewater go? What's inside the tank?

The most important part of the toilet is a pipe called the **siphon**. Without it, your poop would never leave your bathroom. If you look into your toilet bowl, the hole in the bottom is the top opening of the siphon.

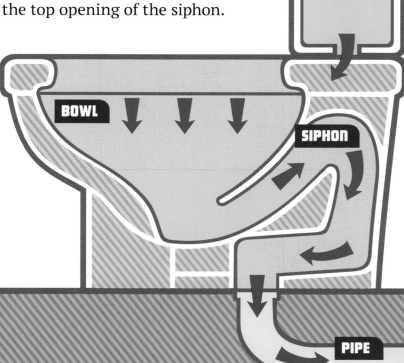

TANK

BOWL

SIPHON

PIPE

A toilet's flushing performance is what matters most. On many toilets, the handle is connected to a chain on the inside of the tank. When you flush, the chain pulls up the **flush valve** inside the tank. The flush valve keeps the clean water inside the tank until it is time to flush. The water is ready and waiting to wash away your waste. After you do your business and flush the toilet, the valve releases the water, and it floods the toilet bowl. That rush of water really gets the siphon going. The siphon sucks the water and waste from the toilet bowl down to the sewer below.

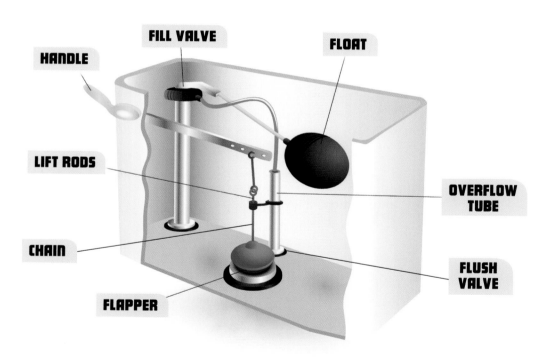

HANDLE

FILL VALVE

FLOAT

LIFT RODS

OVERFLOW TUBE

CHAIN

FLUSH VALVE

FLAPPER

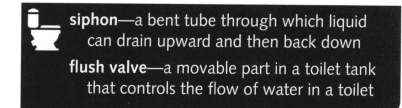

siphon—a bent tube through which liquid can drain upward and then back down

flush valve—a movable part in a toilet tank that controls the flow of water in a toilet

Toilet Tanks

The tank located in the upper part of the toilet holds about 2 gallons (7.5 liters) of clean water. Many toilets have a plastic ball called a float, which is found in the tank. When you flush, the clean water empties out of the tank into the toilet bowl. The float falls to the bottom of the tank. This opens a valve that lets clean water pour back into the tank. The flush valve goes down once the tank fills up with clean water again. After the float reaches the top of the tank, the tank is full. Your toilet is now ready to flush again. This entire process usually takes less than a minute. You can tell when the toilet tank is full because the toilet will stop making noise.

FACT The National Energy Policy Act of 1995 requires new toilets to use 1.6 gallons (6 liters) of water or less per flush. But many homes still have older toilets that use up to 6 gallons (23 liters). That's a lot of extra water!

GURGLE BE GONE

Have you ever heard your toilet making weird noises? It might mean that something is not working properly on the inside of the tank. If that's the case, your toilet tank might be constantly filling up with water. This will cause your water bill to go up. If the flush valve doesn't close right, you could be wasting water without realizing it. A toilet that leaks just 0.003 ounces per minute will waste 139 gallons (526 liters) in a year.

Tube-u-lar Toilet Features

Toilets have a lot of different parts that all need to be working properly in order for the toilet to run smoothly. The refill and overflow tube work together to keep water in the tank and not on your bathroom floor. After the toilet flushes, some water goes down the refill tube and starts to fill up the tank with clean water. The rest goes through the overflow tube into the bowl. This refills the bowl slowly.

As the water in the tank rises, the float does too, telling the water to stop running. But what would happen if the float became detached or the flush valve got stuck? You might walk into a bathroom with toilet water all over the floor, right? Nope! The overflow tube is there to prevent that from happening. It tunnels any extra water into the toilet bowl, keeping your floors dry.

This might happen if your toilet didn't have an overflow tube. Yuck!

Your toilet is one of the most amazing features in your home, but it also has the dirtiest job. Your bodily waste goes into the toilet, as does the waste of everyone else who lives in your home. The average person poops once a day and releases 2 pints (0.9 liters) of urine a day. How many people live in your house? How many toilets do you have? This might give you an idea of just how much waste your toilet has to handle.

Your toilet gets used a lot. It's a good idea to occasionally make sure the inside pieces are all working properly.

Toilet Flow Chart

1. Pushing down on the outside handle pulls the chain attached to the flapper, which releases the flush valve.

2. About 2 gallons (7.6 liters) of water rush from the tank into the bowl, and then the flush valve resets the flapper.

3. The rush of water activates the siphon in the toilet bowl.

4. The level of the water inside the tank falls, and so does the float ball.

5. The water in the tank fills back up. When the float ball reaches a certain level, the refill valve shuts off.

6. The overflow tube keeps your bathroom dry in case any parts in the tank aren't working correctly.

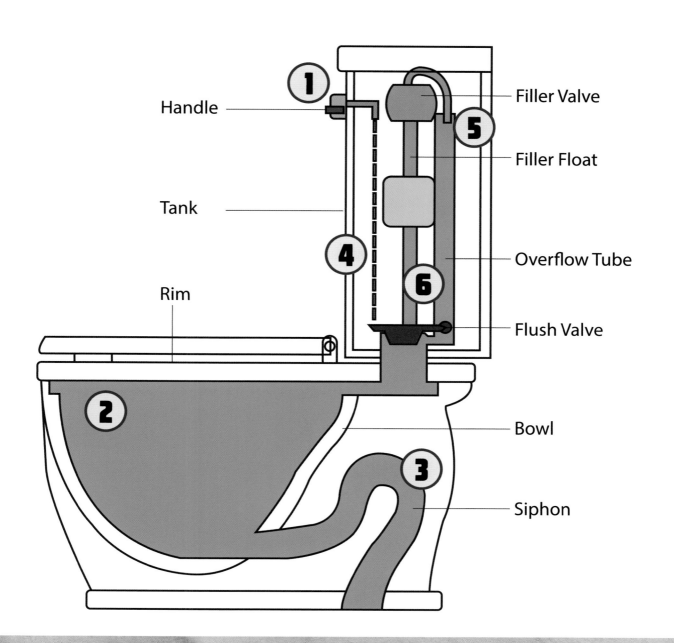

Handle

Tank

Rim

Filler Valve

Filler Float

Overflow Tube

Flush Valve

Bowl

Siphon

CHAPTER 4
FILTHY FACTS AND DIRTY DETAILS

Human waste isn't the only thing that takes a trip through the **U-bend**. Toilet paper does too. But like your toilet, toilet paper hasn't been around very long. Before toilet paper, people wiped with all sorts of things, including newspaper, wool, straw, leaves, grass, moss, and, in a pinch, corncobs. Ancient Romans used a long stick with a sponge on the end. They kept the spongy end in a bucket of salty water when it wasn't being used.

Lucky for us, modern toilet paper was invented in 1857. But it took a little while to catch on and didn't become popular until the 1880s.

Wiping with unfamiliar leaves could lead to rashes or other uncomfortable situations.

U-bend—a U-shaped piece of pipe that holds water in its lower part and prevents unpleasant gases from getting out

QUILTED COLORS

Around the 1950s, people started putting colored toilet paper in their bathrooms. It wasn't softer or more environmentally friendly, but it could match the tile on the floor or the paint on the walls. Scientists realized pretty quickly that the dye used to make these rainbow rolls was harmful to the environment. Some people even had allergic reactions, so this fabulous fad had mostly faded away by the 1990s.

The average person uses about 100 rolls of toilet paper per year.

Bacteria in the Backsplash

Human waste is made up of a combination of things. There's a lot of water and pieces of undigested food. And 8 percent of all solid waste is **bacteria**. Your body pushes out these tiny germs to keep you healthy. These germs end up inside our toilet bowls, but sometimes just a flush isn't enough to make them all disappear.

 bacteria—very small living things that exist all around you and inside you; some bacteria cause disease

Have you ever seen toilet water splash up after you flush? Yuck!

Toilets aren't perfect, which means some germy particles hang around. Some toilets have such a powerful flush that toilet water occasionally sprays up into the air. This means that the germs in that water shoot into the air too. To keep this bathroom bacteria from landing on the toilet seat, sink counter, or worse ... your toothbrush, close the toilet lid before you flush. This can help keep germs where they belong.

Going Green

We know that toilets use water to work, and toilets get used a lot. Toilets are the main source of water use in our homes. On average, toilets make up about 30 percent of a home's indoor water usage. Going green in the bathroom can help the environment by conserving water. Find out if your toilet is low-flow and water efficient.

You can also save water by following the rule of "if it's yellow, let it mellow. If it's brown, flush it down." You should still flush urine in public places and at your friends' homes, but maybe not at your own home. Check with your parents first.

BIDET AWAY!

People in European countries often use a **bidet** in addition to a toilet. Many Americans think a bidet is a toilet, but it certainly is not. The bidet was invented in the 1700s in France. It is a sinklike invention that shoots out a stream of water. Bidets are used to clean your bottom after you use the toilet. Some people use a bidet instead of toilet paper.

bidet—a low, sinklike bathroom fixture with a faucet that points up; a bidet is used to wash a person's bottom area

BIDET

TOILET

25

Tanks a Lot

We may not think about it often, but many of us are very lucky to have access to toilets. About 2.5 billion people in the world don't have access to toilets, or if they do they are not very sanitary. The World Toilet Organization has been working to change the fact that so many people are without safe waste disposal. They want every person to be able to have water to drink that isn't full of germs. The World Toilet Organization even created World Toilet Day. Every year on November 19, they work to help people all over the world understand the importance of toilets.

Some places around the world have squat toilets. These toilets are used by squatting instead of sitting.

The proper disposal of human waste helps us stay healthy and keeps water supplies from becoming **contaminated**. Having accessible toilets keeps our world clean, and we should be very thankful for that.

World Toilet Day helps raise awareness for the people in the world who don't have proper toilets or restrooms.

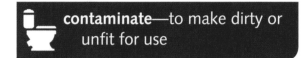

contaminate—to make dirty or unfit for use

TOILETS SAVE LIVES!

WORLD TOILET DAY
19 NOVEMBER
BE THANKFUL YOU HAVE A SAFE AND CLEAN TOILET.
2.5 BILLION PEOPLE IN THE WORLD ARE NOT SO LUCKY.

JOIN THE CONVERSATION
#WORLDTOILETDAY · #OPENDEFECATION · #WECANTWAIT

OPEN DEFECATION   WORLD TOILET DAY

TIMELINE

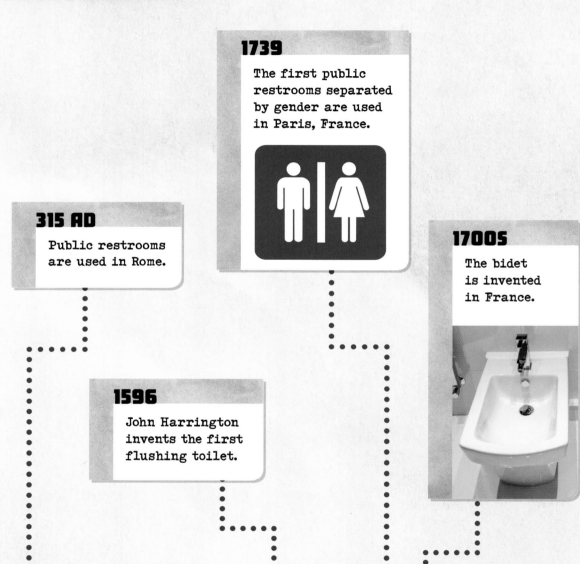

315 AD

Public restrooms are used in Rome.

1739

The first public restrooms separated by gender are used in Paris, France.

1700S

The bidet is invented in France.

1596

John Harrington invents the first flushing toilet.

300 AD   1500   1700

1880S

Thomas Crapper begins selling toilets to the public.

1995

The National Energy Policy Act requires new toilets to use 1.6 gallons (6.1 liters) of water or less per flush.

1857

Modern toilet paper is invented.

1906

William E. Sloan invents the automatic flush toilet.

2001

The World Toilet Organization holds the first World Toiet Day on November 19.

1800

1900

2000

GLOSSARY

bacteria (bak-TEER-ee-uh)—very small living things that exist all around you and inside you; some bacteria cause disease

bidet (bih-DAY)—a low, sinklike bathroom fixture with a faucet that points up; a bidet is used to wash a person's bottom area

cesspool (SESS-pool)—a pit in the ground that holds human waste and other garbage

contaminate (kuhn-TA-muh-nayt)—to make dirty or unfit for use

flush valve (FLUSH VALV)—a movable part in a toilet tank that controls the flow of water in a toilet

siphon (SYE-fuhn)—a bent tube through which liquid can drain upward and then back down

U-bend (yoo-bend)—a U-shaped piece of pipe that holds water in its lower part and prevents unpleasant gases from getting out

READ MORE

Enz, Tammy. *Liquid Planet: Exploring Water on Earth with Science Projects*. Discover Earth Science. North Mankato, Minn.: Capstone Press, 2016.

Resler, Tamara J. *How Things Work: Discover Secrets and Science Behind Bounce Houses, Hovercraft, Robotics, and Everything in Between*. National Geographic Kids. Washington, D.C.: National Geographic, 2016.

INTERNET SITES

Use FactHound to find Internet sites related to this book.

Visit www.facthound.com

Just type in 9781543531145 and go!

 **Super-cool stuff!** Check out projects, games and lots more at **www.capstonekids.com**

CRITICAL THINKING QUESTIONS

1. Toilets use a lot of water. What are some ways you can make sure you are helping conserve water in your home?

2. Why is it important that every person on Earth has access to clean restrooms?

INDEX